Hi! My name is **Amani**. I live with my dad, little sister Jada and cat named Pudge. I love to sing and my favorite subject in school is math. Purple is my favorite color to wear, to color with, and to dress Pudge up in. Pia is my best friend! She loves the color yellow; purple and yellow go together just like we do!

Hey, I'm **Lily**! A couple of years ago, Mom married Steve, so I have two new older siblings—a boy named Warren and a girl named Olivia. Together, my mom and Steve had another kid, my little brother Mikey. Having new people join my family has been a little different and it took me a little while to get used to, but I love it now -except for when Mikey gets into my science experiments! Speaking of science, when we grow-up my best friend, Sebastian, and I want to be scientists!

Hello! My name is **Noah**. My favorite things to do are play video games and go hiking. Right now, I am an only child, but my mom is going to have a baby soon! I don't know if it will be a boy or girl yet, but I'm excited to have a sibling either way...most of the time.

We're the Lopez twins! I'm **Tino** (my real name is Santino, but I like Tino better), I love to do karate, dance, and go on adventures.

And, I'm **Sebastian**! I'm a little taller than Tino even though he's 10 minutes older. My best friend is Lily. We want to be scientists when we grow up! We also have a baby sister, Aly. She's too small to play with now, but we can't wait until she's older!

Hello, my name is **Pia**! I don't have any siblings, but I'm very close to my parents. They are from India and we speak Hindi at home. I love picking flowers with them and playing jump rope with my friend Amani at school. A couple years ago, my dad bought me a violin and I've been playing ever since.

Hi, I'm **Liam**! I love playing sports, but soccer and golf are my favorite. Making friends is the coolest and I love finding new friends wherever I go. I have an older sister named Sarah and a little brother named Owen. We love baking together. Our dog, Pepper, likes to bake too. She's the best at licking up our messes!

Big Emotions, Seeds of Faith
© 2020 by Pam Bowers and Kim Bowers

Written by Pam and Kim Bowers
Illustrated by Nadia Ronquillo

Published in La Vergne, Tennessee by Ingramspark

Scripture quotations marked (ICB) are taken from the International Children's Bible®. Copyright © 1986, 1988, 1999, 2015 by Thomas Nelson. Used by permission. All rights reserved. Scripture quotations marked (NIV) are taken from the Holy Bible, New International Version®, NIV®. Copyright © 1973, 1978, 1984, 2011 by Biblica, Inc.TM Used by permission of Zondervan. All rights reserved worldwide. www.zondervan.com The "NIV" and "New International Version" are trademarks registered in the United States Patent and Trademark Office by Biblica, Inc.TMScripture quotations marked (NLT) are taken from the Holy Bible, New Living Translation, copyright ©1996, 2004, 2015 by Tyndale House Foundation. Used by permission of Tyndale House Publishers, a Division of Tyndale House Ministries, Carol Stream, Illinois 60188. All rights reserved.

Cataloging-in-Publication Data has been applied for and may be obtained from the Library of Congress.

ISBN 978-0-578-71339-7

Printed in USA

Mfr: DSC / LaVergne, TN USA / June 2020

Table of Contents

How to Read this Book

Parents, Families, and Caregivers,

We designed this book to be a tool to help you topically address and maneuver through current daily struggles in your child's life. Different from many of its counterparts, this book does not have a narrative story, but rather is meant to be a platform for conversation between you and your child. It can be used both retrospectively and proactively to help your child prepare for and learn how to handle their big emotions. Additionally, because of the non-narrative style, you can skip around the book in any order as your child needs...you don't need to read it cover to cover! Pick a scenario as the need arises and discuss them one at a time.

The pictures are the driving force of your conversation—feel free to examine every inch of them! Every two pages focus on a single scenario. We suggest you start with the image on the left as it initiates the scenario whereby the character is struggling to work through their big emotions. Then, examine the page on the right. This side revisits the scenario introduced on the left, but shows the character successfully navigating their big emotions. Each image also comes with a series of questions on a sticky note, which serve as a starting guide to help you and your child talk about what you see in each image, the difference in the characters' reactions, and how your child reacts similarly or differently. As you both get comfortable with this inviting learning and sharing style, you will find it easy to eventually think of your own questions to emphasize other characteristics you'd like to work on.

Start with the guiding questions to begin conversations around emotions and responses, and then move to the practical section (the big paragraph on the right page) to enhance your discussion. Each practical section includes various combinations of validation (e.g. "There will be many times in life that you will feel sad--and that's okay"), normalization (e.g., "When we feel this way..."), coping strategies (e.g. "...take a break from the game or your group of friends, take a couple breaths, and talk to God about your anger"), and scripture to help you as caregivers open the lines of communication with your child and help lay a foundation for their faith. These practical sections can also serve as models for you to create your own discussions with your child. Finally, finish with the scripture and prayer. Revisiting these scenarios often can help your child grasp these concepts and apply them as life happens.

The general structure of the book and practical sections come from our collective experiences as a mother, an educator, a coach, and a graduate student. We have found that using this structure and these strategies have been helpful for the children we interact with. As fellow friends, caregivers, and educators, we hope aspects of our model will be helpful for you and yours. Although what we give to you in this book comes from our own personal experiences, we have come to know that scholarly research shares many commonalities. References are available on our website at www.smoothsailingbooks.com.

We wish you all the best in your journey! Remember, growth is not always easy, but it is often worth it in the end.

Your Friends,
Pam & Kim

Sadness

Wow, Liam looks really sad.

He must not want his parents to go see their movie.

8

↖ Discussion Questions
For this page

1. What do you think is happening in the picture?
2. How is Liam feeling?
3. What might he be thinking? What about his face and body show you this?
4. What is Liam doing because of his feelings?
5. How do your face and body look when you feel these things?
6. What do you do when you feel this way?

For that page ↗

7. Revisit questions 1-6 with the other image.
8. What is different about Liam's reaction here than in the other picture?

There will be many times in life that you will feel sad—and that's okay. We can't always control the things in our life, but we have choices we can make when we feel sad. Jesus teaches us to talk to others that we trust about our feelings. People like our grandparents, parents, teachers, and friends are good people to talk to. God put them in our lives so that they can help us understand why we are feeling sad and how to work through our sadness so that we can be joyful again. God also wants us to talk to him. All we have to do is pray!

Psalm 34:18 (NIV) "The Lord is close to the brokenhearted and saves those who are crushed in spirit."

Pray- *"Dear Father God, thank you for this day. Thank you for being close to me and always wanting to hear how my heart is feeling. Please help my heart to become happy again when I feel this way. In Jesus' name I pray, Amen."*

Discussion Questions

For this page

1. What do you think is happening in the picture?
2. How is Pia feeling?
3. What might she be thinking? What about her face and body show you this?
4. What is Pia doing because of her feelings?
5. How do your face and body look when you feel these things?
6. What do you do when you feel this way?

For that page

7. Revisit questions 1-6 with the other image.
8. What is different about Pia's reaction here than in the other picture?

Sometimes finding friends to play with can be hard. Your friends might want to play something different or they might want to play with other people. Either way, it can make you feel sad, mad or both! It's okay for our friends to make those choices. Even though our hearts hurt, we need to allow our friends to be friends with others — and they need to do the same for us. This is what good friendship is all about! So, when we're sad we can pray for God to help our hearts remember that making new friends can be as fun as being with old friends.

Two is **better** than one!

2 Corinthians 1:4 (NLT) "He comforts us in all our troubles so that we can comfort others. When they are troubled, we will be able to give them the same comfort God has given us."

Pray- "Dear Father God, thank you for this day. Thank you for always being there to make me feel better when I'm sad. Please help me to be a friend to others the same way you are to me. In Jesus' name I pray, Amen."

Discussion Questions

For this page

1. What do you think is happening in the picture?
2. How is Noah feeling?
3. What might he be thinking? What about his face and body show you this?
4. What is Noah doing because of his feelings?
5. How do your face and body look when you feel these things?
6. What do you do when you feel this way?

For that page

7. Revisit questions 1-6 with the other image.
8. What is different about Noah's reaction here than in the other picture?

When people say unkind things, it can really hurt our feelings. We might want to cry, be embarrassed, or be mean back. We may even want to change how we look or what we like to fit in. If we let what others say tell us who we should be, then we will never be ourselves. What God thinks of you is always more important than what others think of you. God made you special! All your likes and dislikes, favorites and least favorites are special things that God gave to you when he made you. God loves you for exactly who you are!

Psalms 139:14a (ICB) "I praise you because you made me in an amazing and wonderful way."

Pray- *"Dear Father God, thank you for this day. If something happens today where someone hurts my feelings, please help me to remember the way that you think of me and all of the special ways that you made me, me! In Jesus' name I pray, Amen."*

Anger

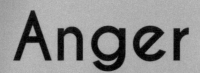

Hey, that's mine!

Give it back!

I'd be mad, too, if someone took my yarn ball.

Discussion Questions

For this page

1. What do you think is happening in the picture?
2. How is Amani feeling?
3. What might she be thinking? What about her face and body show you this?
4. What is Amani doing because of her feelings?
5. How do your face and body look when you feel this way?
6. What do you do when you feel this way?

For that page

7. Revisit questions 1-6 with the other image.
8. What is different about Amani's reaction here than in the other picture?

Sharing is not always easy, especially if we need to share something we really love. We might think that the other person might break it or ruin it, but if it's something your parents would be okay with you sharing, then you should share it! Everything we have is really God's, so if we really think about it, God is actually sharing it with us! Isn't it cool that God shares with you? Knowing that God is sharing with us, will help our hearts want to do the same for others because we know how fun it is to be shared with.

Hebrews 13:16 (ICB) "Do not forget to do good to others. And share with them what you have. These are the sacrifices that please God."

Would you like a turn?

I know you want to play, too. How about we take turns?

Pray- "Dear Father God, thank you for this day. Thank you for all of the cool things that I get to do and get to have. You are so good at sharing and giving! Please help my heart to want to share just like how you share with me. In Jesus' name I pray, Amen."

Discussion Questions

For this page

1. What do you think is happening in the picture?
2. How is Tino feeling?
3. What might he be thinking? What about his face and body show you this?
4. What is Tino doing because of his feelings?
5. How do your face and body look when you feel this way?
6. What do you do when you feel this way?

For that page

7. Revisit questions 1-6 with the other image.
8. What is different about Tino's reaction here than in the other picture?

16

Sometimes it doesn't feel good to be told that what we're doing is wrong, but what we need to remember is that the truth is helpful. Hearing the truth helps us grow and learn. Whether we are in karate class, at school, or at home, we need to make sure that we are listening and obeying. Jesus calls us to follow the rules and to respect the people he put in charge. When we listen to the truth, it helps our minds and bodies grow and even keeps us and others safe!

HI-YA!

Proverbs 19:20 (ICB) " Listen to advice and accept correction. Then in the end you will be wise."

Pray- *"Dear Father God, thank you for this day. My heart does not feel happy when I get corrected. Please help me to remember that when this happens, it will help me do better. Thank you for giving me people who want to help me grow. In Jesus' name I pray, Amen."*

Discussion Questions

For this page

1. What do you think is happening in the picture?
2. How is Lily feeling?
3. What might she be thinking? What about her face and body show you this?
4. What is Lily doing because of her feelings?
5. How do your face and body look when you feel this way?
6. What do you do when you feel this way?

For that page

7. Revisit questions 1-6 with the other image.
8. What is different about Lily's reaction here than in the other picture?

When others do something wrong, it can make us feel angry. We have the choice to be mad about what others are doing or we can try to understand why they did what they did. When you feel this way, take a break from the game or your group of friends, take a couple breaths, and talk to God about your anger. God wants us to be slow to get angry. Taking a minute to do this allows us to help others make better choices, so that everyone can play together kindly.

James 1:19 (ICB) "My dear brothers, always be willing to listen and slow to speak. Do not become angry easily."

When you land on this square, then you get to move forward two spaces.

Oh! That's how you play.

Pray- "Dear Father God, thank you for this day. God, please help me to speak nicely and be slow to get angry when I play or do things with other people. A lot of people are very kind to me. Please help me to be kind like them when I help others. In Jesus' name I pray, Amen."

Moodiness

But, I don't want to take a nap!

A little cat nap wouldn't hurt...

Discussion Questions

For this page

1. What do you think is happening in the picture?
2. How is Amani feeling?
3. What might she be thinking? What about her face and body show you this?
4. What is Amani doing because of her feelings?
5. How do your face and body look when you feel this way?
6. What do you do when you feel this way?

For that page

7. Revisit questions 1-6 with the other image.
8. What is different about Amani's reaction here than in the other picture?

Sometimes we don't know what is best for us, especially when what is best is not what we want to do. Our bodies can make us feel cranky when we are tired. We might not want to do things or we might cry. This is our body's way of asking us to rest. When we feel this way, playing with our friends, watching TV, or playing a videogame may seem way more fun, but it's not going to give our body the rest that it needs. God showed us how important it is to rest when he rested after having so much fun creating the Earth, its animals, and Adam and Eve!

Okay, I'm a little tired.

Can I watch my show when I wake up?

Genesis 2:3 (NIV) "Then God blessed the seventh day and made it holy, because on it he rested from all the work of creating that he had done."

Woo Hoo!

Naptime!

Pray- *"Dear Father God, thank you for this day. Right now playing sounds like a lot more fun than resting, but I can feel my body telling me that I should rest. Please help me to rest like you did. In Jesus' name I pray, Amen."*

21

Discussion Questions
For this page
1. What do you think is happening in the picture?
2. How is Liam feeling?
3. What might he be thinking? What about his face and body show you this?
4. What is Liam doing because of his feelings?
5. How do your face and body look when you feel this way?
6. What do you do when you feel this way?
For that page
7. Revisit questions 1-6 with the other image.
8. What is different about Liam's reaction here than in the other picture?

Waiting is not easy, especially when you are waiting on food. Your tummy might hurt, you might feel a little shaky, or you might feel annoyed; this is your body's way of reminding you to have something to eat. When you feel this way, you need to try your best to be patient while you wait for your food. Asking for a small snack using our kindest words is a good way to help our tummies calm down and help us be kinder while we wait. God calls us to not act on our feelings, but to find ways to be joyful and happy while we wait.

Can we have some apple slices while we wait?

Okay Mom!

My tummy is grumbling a lot!

Fifteen more minutes and then your pizza will be ready!

Save me a slice!

Romans 12:12 (NIV) "Be joyful in hope, patient in affliction (hard times), faithful in prayer. " (additions ours).

Pray- *"Dear Father God, thank you for this day. Please help me to find ways to be patient and happy when my body is telling me to eat some food. Thank you for giving me the food that my body needs. In Jesus' name I pray, Amen."*

Discussion Questions

For this page

1. What do you think is happening in the picture?
2. How is Noah feeling?
3. What might he be thinking? What about his face and body show you this?
4. What is Noah doing because of his feelings?
5. How do your face and body look when you feel this way?
6. What do you do when you feel this way?

For that page

7. Revisit questions 1-6 with the other image.
8. What is different about Noah's reaction here than in the other picture?

When we are doing something we love, it can be hard to put it away and listen to our parents. Obeying, while it might not be what we want to do, will end up making our hearts happy because we are pleasing God and our parents. Often, we are asked to do things because it is what is best for us. If we trust our parents and God that they only ask us to do what is good for us, then it makes obeying easier.

Exodus 20:12 (NLT) *"Honor your father and mother. Then you will live a long, full life in the land the LORD your God is giving you."*

Okay, Mom!

Coming!

I'll be right behind you!

Pray- "Dear Father God, thank you for giving me parents that help me grow and learn. I know that they are not here just to boss me around, but to help me learn to be more like you. Please help my heart to want to listen and obey the first time. In Jesus' name I pray, Amen."

Shyness

↖ Discussion Questions

For this page

1. What do you think is happening in the picture?
2. How is Lily feeling? What might she be thinking?
3. What about her face and body show you this?
4. What is Lily doing because of her feelings?
5. How do your face and body look when you feel this way?
6. What do you do when you feel this way?

For that page ↗

7. Revisit questions 1-6 with the other image.
8. What is different about Lily's reaction here than in the other picture?

Meeting new people is not always fun. We can feel nervous, worried, or embarrassed. It is important to recognize that we feel these things when we meet new people because it is very possible that the person we are meeting feels the same things, too! Instead of giving in to our emotions or feelings, God wants us to think about how the other person is feeling. If we try our best to make them feel more comfortable, everyone will walk away feeling happier.

Philippians 2:3 (ICB) "When you do things, do not let selfishness or pride be your guide. Be humble and give more honor to others than to yourselves."

Pray- "Dear Father God, thank you for this day. I pray that when I get to meet new people, you will help me think of ways to make them feel comfortable instead of only thinking about how I feel. In Jesus' name I pray, Amen."

Class, this is Tino and Sebastian.

They are our new students.

Those kids look **pretty nice!**

I wish Sebastian would look up.

Discussion Questions
For this page
1. What do you think is happening in the picture?
2. How is Sebastian feeling?
3. What might he be thinking? What about his face and body show you this?
4. What is Sebastian doing because of his feelings?
5. How do your face and body look when you feel this way?
6. What do you do when you feel this way?
For that page
7. Revisit questions 1-6 with the other image.
8. What is different about Sebastian's reaction here than in the other picture?

Meeting new kids is not always our favorite thing to do. We like our old friends or we like our family better. At the same time, we need to be willing to meet new friends because our old friends might not always be there. Sometimes they move, sometimes we move, or sometimes we're just not at the same place, but change can be fun. You never know what cool people you'll get to meet! God also calls us to love other people how we would like to be loved. What would make you feel loved if you were meeting someone new?

Mark 12:31 (NIV) "The second is this: 'Love your neighbor as yourself.' There is no commandment greater than these."

Atta Boy!

Give them the old, "smile and wave."

Pray- *"Dear Father God, thank you for the awesome day you have given me. I don't know who I will get to meet today, but you do! I pray that you will help me love others how I like to be loved. In Jesus' name I pray, Amen."*

Worry

Grandpa is going to stay at the hospital for a little while, so that the doctors can take care of him.

But, when will he be better?

What if he never leaves?

Hospitals seem a little scary, but...

Discussion Questions

For this page

1. What do you think is happening in the picture?
2. How is Amani feeling?
3. What might she be thinking? What about her face and body show you this?
4. What is Amani doing because of her feelings?
5. How do your face and body look when you feel this way?
6. What do you do when you feel this way?

For that page

7. Revisit questions 1-6 with the other image.
8. What is different about Amani's reaction here than in the other picture?

Not knowing exactly what will happen or how things will happen can make us feel worried. When we feel this way, we often ask a lot of "What if" questions. Not being able to answer these questions can make us feel worse! The good news is that we can change the way we think about what is worrying us. God helps us with our worries by telling us to think of things that are true, good, and helpful. So, instead of asking the "What if" questions, start thinking of things that you know are true. When we think this way, it will help calm our hearts and give us courage.

Phillippians 4:8 (NIV) "Finally, brothers, whatever is true, whatever is noble, whatever is right, whatever is pure, whatever is lovely, whatever is admirable — if anything is excellent or praiseworthy — think about such things."

Pray- *"Dear Father God, thank you for my family and my friends. I feel worried for them and my mind is making me ask a lot of "What if" questions. Please take care of them and give them the help they need. Please help my heart to trust in you. In Jesus' name I pray, Amen."*

31

Discussion Questions

For this page

1. What do you think is happening in the picture?
2. How is Liam feeling?
3. What might he be thinking? What about his face and body show you this?
4. What is Liam doing because of his feelings?
5. How do your face and body look when you feel this way?
6. What do you do when you feel this way?

For that page

7. Revisit questions 1-6 with the other image.
8. What is different about Liam's reaction here than in the other picture?

When we get worried, our minds may think about all of the bad things that could happen. Just because we think bad things might happen, doesn't mean that we have to believe them! A broken arm might really just be bruised; a forever-lost toy might just be under the couch. To keep ourselves from believing these ideas, we can pause and ask ourselves if we know these things are happening or if we just think they are. After we do this, we can pray to God about our feelings. God says that if we tell him about our worries, he will help our hearts be peaceful.

I wonder what the doctor will say.

Let's pray together.

Philippians 4:6 (NLT) "Don't worry about anything; instead, pray about everything. Tell God what you need, and thank him for all he has done."

Pray- *"Dear Father God, thank you for all of the amazing things you have given me. Right now, I am worried. I need your help to take care of what is going on around me. Please give my heart peace and help me to be happy. In Jesus' name I pray, Amen."*

Fearfulness

> When will we be on the ground?

> What if the wind gets worse?

> Woah!

> This wind is sure bumpy!

Discussion Questions

For this page

1. What do you think is happening in the picture?
2. How is Pia feeling?
3. What might she be thinking? What about her face and body show you this?
4. What is Pia doing because of her feelings?
5. How do your face and body look when you feel this way?
6. What do you do when you feel this way?

For that page

7. Revisit questions 1-6 with the other image.
8. What is different about Pia's reaction here than in the other picture?

Flying on airplanes, riding on trains, going on roller coasters, singing on stage — there are a lot of things that can make us fearful. We cannot fly the plane, control the weather, or decide how other people will respond to us, but you know who is big enough to take care of all those things? GOD! God allows us to be fearful, because it can help us be aware of what is around us. However, if we give into that fear, it can keep us from doing fun and awesome things. We can feel free and happy knowing that God is in control.

Romans 8:28 (NIV) " And we know that in all things God works for the good of those who love him, who have been called according to his purpose."

Pray- "Dear Father God, thank you for always listening. God, right now I am feeling scared about some things. I am not able to control what is going on, but I know that you are. I pray that you will take control and take care of me. In Jesus' name I pray, Amen."

Discussion Questions

For this page
1. What do you think is happening in the picture?
2. How is Lily feeling?
3. What might she be thinking? What about her face and body show you this?
4. What is Lily doing because of her feelings?
5. How do your face and body look when you feel this way?
6. What do you do when you feel this way?

For that page
7. Revisit questions 1-6 with the other image.
8. What is different about Lily's reaction here than in the other picture?

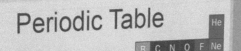

Periodic Table

Shadows and the dark can be very scary. We cannot see what is in front of us, so our minds can trick us into thinking things are there that actually are not. It is okay to ask for help when we feel scared, because others can help us figure things out. God is always there to help us, too. He tells us that he will fight for us! No made-up monster is too big for God. We need only to trust God and let him take care of the scary things we think we see.

Okay, Sparkles.

I know that shadow looks an awful lot like a monster.

But I know that God will take away all of the monsters, so we can just close our eyes and go back to sleep.

Exodus 14:14 (NLT) "The Lord himself will fight for you. Just stay calm."

Pray- *"Dear Father God, right now, I am feeling scared and I need your help to calm down. Thank you for being my big God and for being strong enough to take care of me! In Jesus' name I pray, Amen."*

Discussion Questions

For this page

1. What do you think is happening in the picture?
2. How is Noah feeling?
3. What might he be thinking? What about his face and body show you this?
4. What is Noah doing because of his feelings?
5. How do your face and body look when you feel this way?
6. What do you do when you feel this way?

For that page

7. Revisit questions 1-6 with the other image.
8. What is different about Noah's reaction here than in the other picture?

Big bugs and creepy crawlies are really cool to some kids, but to many they are very scary. If you see one, you may be afraid that it will hurt you. While we still need to be careful around these creatures, we don't need to be scared. God calls us to have self-control, which means to stop and think before we act. Using self-control, we do not hit a bee if it lands on us, kick away a snake that's in our path, or chase away a big bird. Instead, we slowly walk away and tell an adult. Doing this keeps both us and others safe.

2 Timothy 1:7 (NIV) "For God gave us a spirit not of fear but of power and love and self-control."

Mom, be careful.

There's a big spider by you.

I'm so glad I'm in this bowl right now.

Pray- "Dear Father God, before I go out on my day, I pray that you will help me have self-control. If I see a creepy crawly or scary animal, help me to remember that you have given me the power to make good choices so that I can be safe. In Jesus' name I pray, Amen."

Written by Pam and Kim Bowers
Illustrated by Nadia Ronquillo

About the Authors:

Pam and Kim Bowers are a mother-daughter writing team. Pam is a World Top 50 Master Junior Golf Instructor with a passion for child character development. Kim holds a B.A. in Psychology and an M.Ed. in Curriculum & Instruction, Elementary Education. She is currently working on her doctoral studies in School Psychology.

Together they share a rich history in growing in Christ as mother and daughter, disciples, and servant-leaders in his Kingdom with a best-friendship forged by God. Their life experiences, adventures, and God-given talents lend a unique and practical perspective in creating tools to help support God's children and their parents/care-givers.

Visit us at www.smoothsailingbooks.com and @smoothsailingbooks on Instagram.

About the Illustrator:

Nadia Ronquillo is a children's book illustrator, visual development artist and content creator from Ecuador. After receiving her Bachelor's in Graphic Design and Audiovisual Production, she started freelancing as a children's book illustrator and collaborating remotely as a visual development artist with studios in Latin America. She is now developing a tv series show for kids.

For more, visit www.nadiaronquilloart.com and @nadiaronquilloart on Instagram.

Hide and Seek

Find me

Hey! My name is **Swish**. I belong to Noah. I love swimming in my bowl and watching Noah play video games.

Hi, I'm **Pudge**. I live with Amani and her family. My favorite thing to do is take naps. I love Amani and Jada, even if they put me in crazy outfits sometimes.

Hey, I'm **Tut**!
A simple turtle, living his best life!
Lily and her family take good care of me. I
love watching Lily do her experiments — she
has the craziest ideas!

Hi! My name is **Chirp**! I'm a bird who
loves to travel, hang out in trees, and watch
my favorite kids learn and grow.

Hello, I'm **Pepper**. Liam and his family
are my favorite people. I love helping Liam
and his siblings bake — especially when they
drop icing onto the floor.

CPSIA information can be obtained
at www.ICGtesting.com
Printed in the USA
BVHW022148141120
592823BV00001B/1